See. Hear. Touch. Taste. Smell.

That's how we find out about the world around us!

We see
with our eyes.

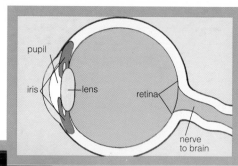

pupil

iris — lens

retina

nerve
to brain

Seeing is how we find out the color, size, shape, and movement of things around us.

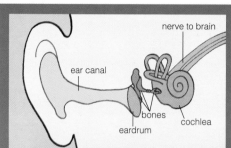

ear canal

nerve to brain

bones

eardrum

cochlea

We hear with our ears.

Hearing is how we find out about the sounds around us.

We touch with our fingers and skin.

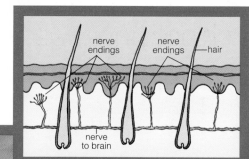

Touching is how we find out
how things feel around us.

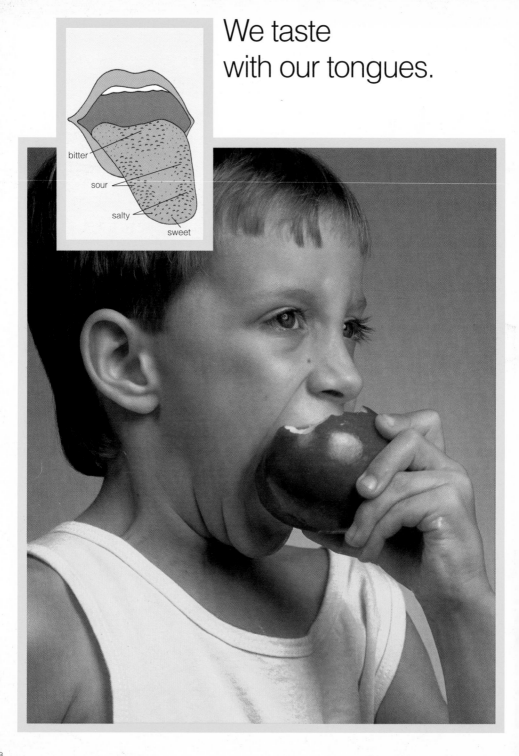

We taste
with our tongues.

bitter

sour

salty

sweet

Tasting is how we find out about the foods around us.

We smell
with our noses.

nerve to brain

nerve fibers

nasal cavity

nostril

Smelling is how we find out
about the odors around us.

We often see and hear at the same time.

Sometimes
we use more
than two senses.

And sometimes we use all five senses!